The Five Emanations

Aligning the Modern Mind with the Ancient Soul

William Douglas Horden

DEDICATION

To My Teachers
Everywhere:

There Is No Succession
Where There Is But A Single Generation

CONTENTS

ACKNOWLEDGMENTS

With Gratitude for the
Unstinting Support and Encouragement
of my lifelong ally,
Dr. Bruce Eichelberger

FOREWORD

THE YOKE OF MEMORY AND UNDERSTANDING

I was born in a cemetery and, to this day, I still have trouble telling the living from the dead.

This doesn't mean my childhood was dark or foreboding.

Not in the least.

Indeed, because my father was the caretaker, I was given free rein of the grounds from the time I could walk. My earliest memories are of wandering manicured lawns, over soft hills of flowering trees and down alongside an ornamental lake with its exotic geese, listening to the stories of the living souls still lingering by their graves. It was a bright timeless dream, the kind that can only exist before one knows anything of death.

It was, in other words, an utterly enchanting beginning that prepared me well for the events to come. Enchanting and, at the same time, paradoxical.

For I was aware from an early age that although visitors came to whisper in hushed tones to the marble headstones, they invariably left without hearing a word of reply. This was a source of confusion at first, since I hadn't yet realized that not everyone could hear the voices of the souls of the deceased.

1

I look back on those days and try to remember how I saw the world before I understood it. I do know that it took me a while to understand that the visitors who came to the cemetery were not just headstones that could come and go as they pleased. Odd as this sounds today, it hints at the reason I've had trouble telling the living from the dead: from the very beginning, I have heard the voices of souls speaking, not just from the grave but from within the living, as well.

And they have not ever sounded any different to my ear.

In a poetic way, I suppose I still see people as headstones. And the world as a cemetery.

This doesn't mean I see the world as dark or foreboding.

Not in the least.

Indeed, because the soul speaks independently of the living body—and often in a surprisingly different voice than that of the personality—the entire world is filled with the song of souls moving between lives, a secret garden of sheer mountains and lush valleys and dancing rivers flying toward moon-inspired seas. It is a bright timeless dream, the kind that exists once one knows anything of immortality.

I bring up immortality because the dead see the living as twofold beings—one, the personality that's convinced it is the sum of the body's experiences and, the other, the immortal soul moving from body to body, lifetime to lifetime. Of course, many of the dead see themselves the same way: if they still haunt this world, it is because they have not yet stopped identifying with their body's personality and remembered their immortal self.

So I have learned to listen with two ears: even as I keep one ear attuned to the voice of the personality, I keep the other attuned to the voice of the soul.

And they have very seldom sounded the same.

To repeat: all my life, I have heard the voices of souls speaking, not just from the grave but from within the living, as well.

What exactly have I heard?

First and foremost, it is the souls of the living sighing for freedom from the constraints of society that the personality has accepted.

Even as the personality speaks of the love, acceptance, recognition, and success offered by social conformity, the soul speaks of meaningful purpose, lifelong allies, endless discovery, and collaboration on the widest scale. Even as the personality speaks the language of self-interest and self-importance, the soul speaks the language of benefiting the whole and the sacredness of everything. Even as the personality speaks of wrong roads and dead ends, the soul speaks of homecoming and metamorphosis.

So I have learned to listen to the personality and the soul at the same time.

And I have rarely heard them echoing one another.

As it turns out, there are so very few individuals whose personality and soul speak the same language. Just as I once watched people whisper to gravestones without hearing the soul's reply, I have watched all my life as people talk to themselves without hearing their soul's reply. Mistaking the personality for their true self, they so occupy their attention with the personality's habitual thoughts, feelings, and memories that there is no room left for the soul's gentle call to seek peace and well-being for all.

I have also heard the souls of the dead sighing for freedom — freedom from the compulsive memories of their last lifetime. Because the personality is the sum of the body's experiences, it cannot conceive of the bodiless immortality of the soul. Although the soul hears everything the personality says, most personalities go their whole life without ever hearing the pure song of light continually pouring forth from the soul. Taught about the soul in church or books, the personality imagines what it might feel like to experience it and so interacts with its imagination rather than its actual soul.

Sadly, this failed communion then persists after the death of the body. Even as the personality recounts the memories of its body's experiences, the soul recounts its understanding of the perennial truth. Even as the personality laments the loss of its bodily sensations, the soul laments its inability to influence the living more profoundly. Even as the personality relives its past lifetime as though still alive, the soul relives its deathless communion with all other souls.

I have learned, in other words, that nothing is as uncommon as a conscientious communion of personality and soul. Nor is anything as important. All that we come into contact with reminds us that it is impossible to fully experience each moment without the shared presence of the personality and the soul.

So I have also learned to yoke my personality and soul in the moment-by-moment, step-by-step, breath-by-breath, plowing of the field of meaning.

But what exactly was it all preparing me for?

For my death, of course.

I didn't see it coming but it's obvious in hindsight: by learning to fully experience each moment of living, I was really learning to fully experience the moment of dying.

I was fully awake when my heart stopped beating and my last breath passed my lips.

Without any real warning, a genetic time bomb went off and my body's time came to an end. The moment of death was upon me at age fifty-three and I found it a curious thing indeed. People around me grew quite excited but an untroubled calm came over me, carrying me further and further away from the scene, as if moving me to an invisible but familiar place just sideways to where my body lay. The sirens of the ambulance were soft and melodic, the questions of the emergency room doctors sounded like a different language.

Minutes after they placed me on the emergency room table and fit an oxygen mask over my face, I felt my heart stop beating and I sighed my last breath. There was the briefest pause while my personality puzzled that I did not gasp for breath nor seem concerned that my body had just died—and then it was suddenly cradled in my soul and I was catapulted, for that is the only word for it, catapulted, wide awake, out of my body and into the Universal Sphere of Communion.

My whole life, it turned out, had been practice for the moment of dying: my soul stepped forward, speaking reassuringly about how it had been through this so many times before. While my personality went mute in the face of

5

the Unknown, my soul catapulted into It with one last sigh of joy and gratitude, *What a glorious Creation!*

I was fully awake when I entered the Sphere of Universal Communion.

How do I know that is its true name? I do not. I am not even sure it's possible for it to have one single true name. But the Sphere of Universal Communion is what I saw and what I felt and it's the only true name I can imagine, the only one I can use to describe it at all.

It is a sphere of light, but light that is aware. Not something so much seen—since we have no physical eyes without a body—as sensed. Something like the warmth of sunlight even when your eyes are squeezed shut. But with the additional sense of someone present, close by, their attention resting on the edges of your awareness gently. An aware light that is both the substance and the medium of communion within its own spherical spaciousness. An aware light that creates and sustains the possibility of shared awareness on a universal basis. Within its infinite spatiality.

I was fully awake when I realized I was myself a sphere of communion.

A sphere of aware light.

Surrounded by an infinite number of other spheres of aware light.

What I *saw*, then, is that the Sphere of Universal Communion is an infinite space of aware light that is occupied by all the individual spheres of aware light that ever have or ever will exist. As if it were the One Mind, occupied by all the individual Ideas it ever has or ever will conceive. Or the timeless, dimensionless, Oversoul, occupied by all the individual souls that ever have or ever will enter the realm of time, space, and personality. As I said, I do not pretend to know what it's true name is, but the relation between the Whole and its parts—and between parts and parts—this I know and can still see with diamond clarity.

What can I still see of that bodiless state?

Each of us, as an individual sphere of communion is the embodiment of two complementary halves: Understanding and Memory. While Understanding is the principal characteristic of our soul, Memory is the principal characteristic of our personality. Understanding is our individual portion of the limitless Knowledge of the One Soul, the evolving insight we possess into the Way of the One, our individual spark of immortality. Memory, on the other hand, is the accumulated impressions of all the lifetimes we recall, the sum of all the personalities we have yoked to our soul, our enduring storehouse of mortal treasures.

Each of us, as an individual sphere of aware light, then, dwells in the Universal Sphere of Communion, a unique fusion of soul and personality, Understanding and Memory. After the death of the body, the soul catapults back to the Universal Sphere of Communion. If it is not yoked to the personality at that time, then it returns without any memory of that lifetime. It has Understanding, perhaps greatly evolved by its experiences of that lifetime, but no direct Memory. The personality, likewise, must be yoked to the soul at the moment of dying if its Memory is to accompany it to the Sphere of Universal Communion. Otherwise, it wanders without Understanding, lost and confused among all the other disembodied personalities, unaware that they no longer have a body and are only reliving the Memory of their past lifetime.

It is for this reason that it is so important to unite the soul and personality during this lifetime, before the moment of dying arrives.

I was fully awake when I realized that whenever another sphere of aware light came into contact with me, there was an immediate and spontaneous exchange between us of our respective Memory and Understanding. This is why I say we are *spheres of communion*. Because when we come into contact, all that we know and all that we are passes uninhibited between us in a natural and open communion of shared being. Spheres of aware light touch and exchange the totality of their experience and assimilate one another's experience into their own.

So I learned in those moments that all the individual spheres are *reflective of one another*.

I was fully awake when all the individual spheres of communion came into contact with one another at the same time, breaking through every dam of individuality and flooding us all in the totality of our shared being. This is why I say it is the *Sphere of Universal Communion*. Because when all the individual spheres of aware light periodically come into contact at the same time, every individual awareness that ever has or ever will exist is spontaneously and immediately At-One with the One. I cannot say what it is that periodically draws all of us together at the same time but, cause aside, its effect is the complete and overwhelming experience of every drop of awareness in the ocean suddenly merging into the single sea of awareness.

So I learned in those moments that all the individual spheres are *relative to the Whole*.

How did I learn these lessons?

Through my communion with other spheres of communion—and my communion with the Sphere of Universal Communion.

My body was dead for two minutes but for me, the time passed as if it were many years.

Other individual spheres of aware light, many of great depth of Understanding with the Memory of thousands of lifetimes, generously taught me lessons to bring back and place into the stream of time. This book, *The Five Emanations*, presents part of those lessons my teachers feel belong to this era of transformation.

Before you move on to read the body of this book, I would like you to consider one last lesson that I have learned since returning to this realm of the body and its five senses—

Although it is much more difficult to perceive here than in the Sphere of Universal Communion, we are no less spheres of communion here than we are there. Once I had experienced what it feels like to recognize myself as a sphere of aware light in the bodiless state, I had become sensitive enough to perceive myself as that same sphere of communion here with a body. And sensitive enough to recognize that everyone else is a similar sphere of aware light, as well.

Moreover, although it is even more difficult still to perceive the spontaneous and immediate exchange of Understanding and Memory that occurs when we individual spheres of communion come into contact here, it occurs nonetheless, even if not in our conscious awareness.

I have, in other words, been a wayfarer with a body and been a wayfarer without a body and have not ever found any difference.

So what I have learned from birth to death to rebirth is this: just as learning to live is actually preparing to die, it is clear that preparing to die is actually learning to live.

Blessing

Awaken Early
Find Lifelong Allies

THE ART OF LIVING

The great philosophical questions of the ages no longer concern me.

The really essential issue, as it turns out, is much more practical and immediate —

> *What are the moment-to-moment thoughts*
> *we are projecting every day?*

Of all the pressing matters in the world, why should our moment-to-moment thoughts be considered so important? Because *the way we are thinking and feeling all the time forms our relationship with the world.* As we will find as we work with the Five Emanations, our thoughts, emotions and memories are inner actions much like pebbles tossed into a pond. These inner actions ripple out across the inner landscape of the spiritual world we all share, interacting with all the other ripples in the invisible half of our visible world.

The inner world of spirit, after all, is not just inside you and me — it is also the invisible half of all physical matter. And, just as it requires an entire physical universe to support just one planet or even one life, it requires an entire spiritual universe to support just one soul. Moreover, just as our thoughts, emotions and memories have a direct impact on our physical bodies, they also extend into our shared spiritual world to impact the physical world around us. In this sense, the spiritual world can be thought of as the underlying harmony of cause-and-effect that creates form and change in the physical world.

HABIT-THOUGHTS

The sense of "me" that we experience as our private, individual, personality is formed by the thoughts, emotions and memories we habitually fall back into whenever we are not actively engaged with the outer world. This habit-mind is a kind of default stance that we are most familiar with, the stream of consciousness we "hear" by silently "talking to ourselves". We are most familiar with this "me" because we have lived with it our whole life and, although it has changed some over time, those changes are generally made by adding new habits to the old ones. Like new rings of a tree added to the existing ones, it is not so much change as it is new growth in the same old direction. The thoughts we think, the emotions we feel and the memories we relive by habit—these are the components of our individual life-mood, the relatively constant way we have felt about our life since childhood that determines how we respond to what happens to us.

More than that, however, this life-mood—this personal demeanor, this lifelong disposition—pours out of us into the invisible world of cause-and-effect that creates change in the visible world. The long-term effect of these ingrained attitudes is a stagnant relationship with the world around us: *when our moment-to-moment thoughts remain the same, our personal power and success and luck remain the same.* The consistent inner actions we are habitually producing radiate out into the spiritual environment, where they interact with those of others. It is in this realm that we can change our life for the better—*when we change our moment-to-moment thoughts, we change our personal power and success and luck.*

SOUL-THOUGHTS

So, the ripples from our inner actions *emanate* outward from us in a series of concentric circles, just as the ripples from a pebble emanate across the surface of a pond. As we will see, the Five Emanations are inner actions that we *consciously take up* to replace our habitual thoughts, emotions and memories. They are ancient thoughts that evoke new emotions and memories, thereby opening the door for a new moment-to-moment stream of consciousness to pour out of us into the realm of spiritual cause-and-effect.

The Five Emanations are timeless lessons of wisdom that have for ages been used to align the personality with the soul. They attune our personality to the laws of spiritual cause-and-effect, bringing it into harmony with the underlying harmony of the world. By concentrating on the Five Emanations instead of allowing our habit mind to run away with us, we change our relationship to the world—by thinking soul-thoughts instead of personality-thoughts, we rise above the pettiness of self-centeredness that has been holding us back from experiencing our birthright of full personal power, success and luck.

The Five Emanations are, then, soul-thoughts that orient the personality to the compass points of the spiritual landscape. The practice of concentrating on each Emanation in turn evokes more sublime sensitivities and engenders more profound experiences—it allows us, in other words, to respond to events in creative, spontaneous and beneficial ways rather than continuing to react in predictable and habitual ways. By shifting our attention away from the narrow view of the personality's self-interest, we paradoxically make the personality more successful. This occurs because soul-thoughts resonate with the underlying harmony of the spiritual laws of cause-and-effect, thereby unlocking the hidden doors leading to greater personal power, success and luck. In this sense, working with the Five Emanations enhances the way we interact with others and allows us to make new kinds of decisions—not simply more effective ones, but startling and surprising decisions that carry us into a new and more exciting life.

By correctly orienting us within the spiritual realm of cause-and-effect, the Five Emanations transforms our moment-to-moment *inclination* toward what we are about to experience. They allow us to *lean into the coming moment* with a more open-minded, open-hearted and dynamic personality. Instead of leaning into the coming moment with the kind of self-defeating thoughts, emotions and memories that lead us to keep trying the same failed strategies over and over, we find ourselves attuned to the Whole and moving along with it conscientiously.

Ultimately, the primary lesson we learn from the Five Emanations is this: *What we are looking for is not something we wait to learn or understand or receive—it is something that we ourselves produce in our hearts and send forth to shine on the furthest horizons of the spiritual universe.*

THE PRACTICE

Our moment-to-moment thoughts ought to lead to greater personal power, success and luck. But, as suggested in the Foreword, they should also contribute directly to our uniting the soul and the personality during this lifetime.

These are the two most practical and immediate consequences of replacing our habit-thoughts with the soul-thoughts of the Five Emanations.

Habit-thoughts are not so difficult to identify. They are those that come unbidden to dampen our joy of life. They may come in the form of sentences that we have repeated to ourselves for years. They may come in the form of emotions that we have relived for years, the most troubling of which may originate from a time before we learned to talk and so are difficult to ascribe to a specific cause. They may come in the form of memories linked by events that made us feel powerless, ashamed or desperate. But what they all have in common is that they seem to have a mind of their own, intruding without our consciously deciding to entertain them and then taking over our moment-to-moment stream of consciousness to dampen our joy of life.

We consciously take up the practice of the Five Emanations by concentrating on those soul-thoughts with enough force of intent that we replace our habit-thoughts with them. *Because we can entertain only one conscious thought at a time, we can wrest control from habit-thoughts by concentrating on soul-thoughts.*

- To begin with, concentrate on each Emanation for one day, *holding it in your mind by consciously repeating it whenever you are not actively engaged with the outer world*, especially when you notice your habit-thoughts intruding to extinguish your joy of life. Instead of following out your habit-thoughts to their usual endings, interrupt them as soon as they start with that day's Emanation.

In this first stage of the practice, spend a day on each Emanation, repeating the cycle of five for several weeks, using them primarily to interrupt your habit-thoughts.

After you have familiarized yourself with the Emanations as a whole and experienced success in interrupting your habit-mind, move on to the second stage of the practice.

- In the second stage, concentrate on each Emanation for an extended period of time—usually somewhere between three weeks and a month. The point here is to keep the periods of time equal. While you will still use the Emanations to interrupt old habit-thoughts, you *spend more time rolling each Emanation around in your mind*. Delve deeper into its meanings. Move it into the heart so that it unlocks soul-emotions. Follow it into more profound moment-to-moment experiences, allowing it to build new more sublime memories of this lifetime.

At this point, depending on how long you spent on each Emanation, you may want to repeat the second stage. Otherwise, you will proceed to the third stage of the practice.

- In this third stage, you proceed through your daily life, applying each Emanation according to circumstance. This is accomplished by *paying close attention to both your moment-to-moment thoughts, as well as your responses to events around you, and then concentrating on the soul-thought that holds the greatest promise of freeing you to act* with greater personal power, success and luck. One day, old habit-thoughts of worthlessness might arise, for example, and you respond by concentrating on the First Emanation. The same habit-thought might arise another day and you choose to respond by concentrating on the Third Emanation, or the Fourth, etc. Likewise, a situation might arise where you feel under pressure to perform according to others' expectations. Or perhaps a conflict arises that continues unresolved. Or someone betrays your trust. Rather than responding by falling back on old self-defeating habits of thought, emotion and memory, however, you hold to the practice by *concentrating on the Emanation that holds the greatest promise of freeing you to act with the greatest creativity, fortitude and dignity.*

You will know you have mastered the third stage of the practice when you become increasingly aware of the positive changes cropping up in unexpected and surprising ways in your life.

• Having reached the final stage, you continue using the Five Emanations as circumstances require, but now you begin consciously formulating your own personal soul-thoughts to take their place.

From this stage forward, your personality increasingly identifies with the perceptions and intentions of the soul. Your thoughts are clear and inspired. Your emotions are heightened and ennobled. Your memories are a mirror—true and vivid when beheld, gone without a trace when out of mind.

You have recovered your birthright of true freedom, true power, true luck and true charisma.

You have rediscovered the lost secret of the Art of Living.

THE FIVE EMANATIONS

Aligning the Modern Mind with the Ancient Soul

THE FIRST EMANATION

REFLECTION

*As an immortal spirit, are these the thoughts, feelings
and memories I choose for eternity?*

We begin the practice by looking into the mirror of our own
immortality.

With this Emanation, we ask the soul-question that cuts
through all rationalization and self-deception. Only I know
what "these thoughts, feelings, and memories" are. No one
else can condone them or condemn them for me. I alone
know how deep they run, whether they ennoble or demean
me.

I hold up this Emanation so I can look into my own
reflection, in the privacy of my own conscience, and state
unequivocally whether I am pleased with what is passing
through my mind. It requires of me that I answer with a
simple yes or no. It treats me with a seriousness of purpose
that prevents me from resorting to trivial or inauthentic
answers.

Once I move away from the cultural conditioning that holds me to the standard of others' personalities, I find it natural to return to my intuitive sense of the true self whose origins reach back before the womb. Taking my stand here in the immediate sense of my immortal nature, I effortlessly recognize the self-defeating habits of thought, emotion and memory that I do not cherish.

With this beginning, we set off on the path of moment-to-moment immortality. If our eternal awareness does not begin now, after all, when could it possibly begin?

Because how I spend eternity is tied directly to the quality and consistency of my moment-to-moment awareness, it is not something to be put off for another day. Wasting time only allows my self-defeating habits of thought to sink their roots deeper into my moment-to-moment awareness. Returning to the secret garden, I begin by pulling out weeds.

In this sense, it is just like building a house—first, it is necessary to clear the land.

So, the First Emanation affords us a reflection of our moment-to-moment awareness by setting it against the standard of our own eternal well-being—

As an immortal spirit,
are these the thoughts, feelings and memories
I choose for eternity?

Watch your thoughts. Watch your emotions. Watch your memories.

And at every step of the practice, concentrate on the First Emanation, keeping your feet on the path that will allow you to consistently answer irrevocably and resoundingly, *Yes!*

22

THE SECOND EMANATION

FREEDOM

What is most important is not how others are treating me—
What is most important is how I am treating others.

True freedom is not just about freeing ourselves from the control of others in ever more ennobling ways.

It also requires that we learn to exercise ever more ennobling self-control.

Why the emphasis on *ennobling*? Primarily, because the great failures of civilization—war, poverty, hunger, injustice, environmental degradation—all arise from a basic lack of noble intentions and behaviors. None of these inhumane behaviors are possible when people everywhere think, feel and act nobly: what we all really wish to leave to the future generations is a world where these failures have dissolved like night mists in the dawning sunlight of the question, *What shall we build together?* There is no real advancement in human life possible now until our wisdom surpasses our technological achievements and our care for the sacredness of all life surpasses our belief in our divine right to place our own interests ahead of all others. The inevitable Golden Age of Humanity arises from the ashes of ignoble hearts, the phoenix ignites itself with the spark of nobility in each individual's heart.

Closer to home, of course, is the joy of life that we all seek — an uninterrupted sense of buoyancy and light-heartedness that cannot be found in a heart with ignoble thoughts, feelings and memories. It is many times easier to achieve true freedom once we establish the goal of noble thoughts, noble emotions and noble actions. This is the kind of conscientious moment-to-moment awareness that proceeds from the practice of Reflection in the First Emanation: conscientiously uprooting the weeds of ignobility, we are inevitably left with the flowers of nobility.

Because we cannot control how others treat us, we are at their mercy *if we allow ourselves to be unduly influenced by the way they treat us.* We are held hostage by our own reactions so long as we allow others to unduly influence us with their behavior. When others are able to evoke feelings in us *by the way they are treating us,* then we have abdicated our freedom to respond to events as we truly wish. This is an important distinction: we are not talking about having feelings for others — we are talking about others' actions controlling our feelings.

When others are not treating me right, that is their problem. It is something that they have to fix. It is a matter of their own ethics and conscience. There is nothing I can do to force them to act nobly. Even if I am able to force them to change their superficial behavior, I have done nothing to affect their deeper attitudes, so they will predictably continue to treat me as before but in more subtle and difficult-to-define ways. This is another important distinction: this has nothing to do with the fact that others wrong me—this has everything to do with gaining freedom from *feeling* wronged.

It likewise affects the way I deal with being treated well by others. Nothing seems more natural than to bask in the warm sunlight of acceptance, affection and recognition—what could be better? For the developing personality of the infant, obviously, nothing could be better than unconditional love and acceptance. And, of course, what could seem more natural than to take those actions to heart and base one's feelings on such positive regard? But what happens when the infant grows up and begins to express its individuality, especially if that means having different goals and values and behaviors than the parents? What happens to our emotional life when all that positive regard is withdrawn?

Such problems are not isolated to parent-child relations, though. Take for example the situation where one partner in the relationship has an affair. If the other partner has based their sense of identity on the way their partner treats them, then the sense of betrayal causes an intense period of confusion and disorientation. And results in feelings of outrage and righteous indignation that make anger and resentment seem like justifiable responses. But when we enter relationships despite knowing that such things can happen, when we do not base our sense of self on the way the other person treats us, then the other person's actions are matters of their own evolution, their own ethics, their own conscience, and not matters that throw us off balance and into an emotional and spiritual tailspin. This carries over into our relationships with causes and institutions, as well. Patriotism can turn on us as soon as we feel our country is not treating us the way it should. Or our employer, of course: how many fall into depression and disillusion because they invested their sense of self in their work, only to be laid off or mistreated due to a change in policy?

So, the positive, too, can be the bait in the trap. True freedom means achieving mental, emotional and spiritual equilibrium. It means finding the center point of the teeter-totter and not being pulled to one side or the other. This Emanation is about coming to terms with our inability to control how others treat us — and moving on to focus on what we really *can* control.

For many, this is the most difficult step on the path. Convinced that their identity is determined by the relationships they have and by what others think about them, they go to any length to rationalize why the way others treat them is so important. Which raises a third distinction: this Emanation speaks to what is *most* important in life: *it is the key to establishing my relationship to all my relationships*.

The personality will maintain its attitudes and behaviors even when they do not result in the kind of life they are intended to produce. The personality will continue to believe in its over-arching importance despite all evidence to the contrary. The personality will not even recognize its habit of blaming others, let alone give it up, without a fight. All this is because the personality has Memory but not Understanding.

If we do not call the personality's habits into question, if we do not open our hearts to the possibility of a more authentic life based on spiritual freedom, power and good fortune, then we remain mired in self-defeating justifications for continuing on as we are.

To stand alone, one soul face-to-face with the universe, however, is to regain the soul's Understanding: I am *relative* to the One Source and *reflective* of all other souls. This means that what is *most* important is my relationship to the Living Whole. And it means that what is *most* important to others is their relationship to the Living Whole. The ray of light, in this sense, is *relative* to the sun even as it is *reflective* of all the other rays pouring from the same source. I maintain the integrity of my relationship with the Living One by keeping my moment-to-moment awareness filled with noble—and ennobling—thoughts, emotions and memories.

This, of course, is what I *can* control.

How am I treating the other?

Who am I holding in mind, in other words, and how am I treating them in my mind? Whether the person is in front of me or on the other side of the world or not yet born or no longer living—how am I treating them in my mind?

As we move further away from the personality's dependence on others for validation, we move closer to the soul's freedom to respond to others with the universal goodwill pouring from the Source of All Souls. This is the opposite of using the moment-to-moment awareness to suffer needlessly and keep the soul and personality separate: by using the moment-to-moment awareness to align the personality's thoughts with the soul's thoughts, we radiate joy of life and unite the two during this lifetime.

So what *is* the goodwill of the soul? When it comes to the right way of treating others, what *are* the standards to which I ought to hold myself?

Certainly, each of us will continue to find our own way of expressing that goodwill as our Understanding continues to grow and unfold—but, just as certainly, there are certain baseline standards of inner actions we can use as a starting point.

As we will see in the following chapters, the next three Emanations provide us with just such a baseline—and lead us deeper into the transformative nature of the practice.

I know it can sound like a daunting challenge to change your moment-to-moment thinking.

Your personality is so convinced that the habit thoughts running along with your body are *you* that it comes up with any number of reasons why replacing those thoughts is impossible. Even if those reasons can be addressed rationally, there is still an emotional component that is often reticent to admit that it is *already* talking to itself all the time. Repeating the same thoughts over and over, reacting to events in the same habitual way day in and day out, entertaining the same memories, most of which are based on pain and loss—the personality keeps the moment-to-moment awareness overwhelmed with the sense of a personal history in order to maintain the continuity of its artificial identity.

That it is an artificial identity is easy to prove. Imagine that you were born to the same parents on the same day in the same place as you were—but that the next day they moved to central Africa, for example, where you were raised for the next 25 years among a tribe of gentle people still living in harmony with the forest, people who experienced the jungle as alive, who asked permission of the spirit world before they harvested anything and who asked for the spirit world's blessing whenever they undertook any endeavor. Then, after 25 years in such an environment, you returned to live where you do now. *Do you really imagine you would be the same person you are now?*

What the personality does not like to consider is this: if that sense of *you* is so completely determined by external events, then there is no real sense of *you* that the personality has to offer.

Training the personality to voluntarily quiet itself so that the soul's thoughts, emotions and memories might be heard— *that* is why many people find the Second Emanation the most difficult step in the practice. Changing your moment-to-moment thinking, after all, changes *you*.

Replacing habit-thoughts with soul-thoughts allows you to transcend the personality's sense of self and identify with the soul's sphere of awareness. Identifying with the soul instead of the personality attunes you to the Current of Spirit creating form and change in the world, carries you along with it, and assures you true power, true success and true luck.

This voluntarily relinquishing of the personality's will in favor of the One Will is our initiation into the sphere of true freedom.

Abandon the sense of being controlled and you have no need to control how others treat you.

Fill your moment-to-moment awareness with the Second Emanation of Freedom:

What is most important is not how others are treating me—
What is most important is how I am treating others.

THE THIRD EMANATION

POWER

I am a well of happiness,
overflowing into the lives of others.

To the personality, power is the ability to get what it wants or needs. But to the soul, power is the ability to give what others want or need: there is no greater sense of resourcefulness than being able to contribute to the well-being of others.

As we increasingly sense ourselves as spheres of aware light, we become increasingly conscious of coming into contact with other spheres of aware light—and of the exchange of Understanding and Memory that passes between us during such moments of communion. In this way, we realize that we are reaching a turning point: for our entire life, our soul has looked at the world through our eyes but now, we are looking at the world through our soul's eyes. Now we are starting to see others as souls instead of personalities. We are seeing trees and mountains and clouds and animals as souls instead of their outer appearances. We are beginning to *care* about things other than ourselves in ever-deepening ways that startle us with their directness and unavoidable sense of *belonging together*.

To the personality, power is the ability to turn matters to its advantage. But to the soul, power is the ability to turn matters to the advantage of others.

On the surface of things, this seems counterproductive and even self-defeating to the personality. In a world of increasing competition, how can placing the needs of others ahead of our own possibly serve our best interests? If I try to turn things to the advantage of others, what is to keep them from adding fuel to the fire and simply taking the opportunity to take advantage of me? Nice as this idea sounds, isn't it really too idealistic and naive to be practical?

Predictable reactions, to be sure. The first thoughts to leap to the mind of many. But they are questions that fail to take into account that the soul already has enough. Forever. They are questions that assume the soul acts according to the same law of competition that governs the personality's behavior. For the soul, a lifetime is a journey in search of opportunities to create something meaningful with others—not the opportunity to succeed at the expense of others.

We already know that competition doesn't work. Whatever short-term gains might seem to warrant competitive behavior, the long-term results of competition in a competitive environment clearly elicits immediate distrust and even antagonism from others. Competitive behavior evokes fear and anxiety in the personality, since it must be constantly vigilant against the next threat, whether real or imagined.

Competition, in other words, makes us less powerful.

And cooperation makes us more powerful. Even on the level of the personality, it is apparent that we cannot sustain the current cycles of war anymore, let alone the partition of resources in a way that perpetuates hunger and poverty among so many of our peers in this cornucopia of a world.

But on the level of the soul, competition is unthinkable: one part of the whole seeking gain at the expense of another part is experienced as the very mechanism of disease, analogous to a cell turning against the body.

The power to take from others is not true power.

True power is the power to create with others.

All this comes from the simple intention to *be of benefit to the whole*. Rather than training our intention on constantly looking for the opportunity for personal gain or advantage, we train our intention on being of benefit to all.

This is often called *cultivating the pickpocket's view*. Whether in a cafe or walking down the street or standing in a crowded station or relaxing on a beach, the pickpocket's eye is always alert to the opportunity to pick the purse or pockets of his unsuspecting victim. It is this very *constant vigilance* we work to cultivate. If a common thief with the basest motives can achieve such a state of concentration, after all, it cannot be impossible for the rest of us do so. The only difference is that *our eye is always alert to the opportunity to benefit the whole* rather than gain at the expense of others.

The pickpocket is, of course, the personality. It has been trained since childhood to think in terms of keeping what it has and acquiring more without violating its personal ethics. For this reason, much of *The Five Emanations* practice can be thought of as making the pickpocket's view conscious and turning it to the soul's will.

For the soul, all matter and life and spirit are a single body. There is an inherent equality among all the parts, just as all the drops of the ocean are equal. The relationship between all the parts can only be one of respect and honoring the role each plays in the ever-evolving perfection of the whole. This sense of harmonious belonging together is the basis of true happiness. For the soul, there is no more sublime foundation upon which to build than the sense of trust among all devoted to the common purpose of mutual benefit. The heart looses such a sigh of relief upon stepping into that realm where all are buoyed by the universal goodwill emanated by each: the soul cannot hold back its laughter upon returning to that realm where the struggle for survival and dominance has not ever existed in thought or deed.

From the soul's perspective, then, the personality has every right to instinctively feel entitled to happiness, since that is the birthright of each and every part of the whole. This extends well beyond all the other people in the world—or even the future generations. It includes all the animals and plants—not just now, of course, but into the future, as well. It also includes the land and sea, the rivers and mountains, the forests and deserts—the planet itself. Once we sense the soul within all matter and life, no thought can distance us from the reality of the sacredness of everything: our heart opens, unprotected as a raw nerve, to both the bliss of immortality and the suffering of mortality.

It is the paradox of awakening to the dream of the mortal personality that our happiness cannot be divorced from an acute awareness of the confusion and pain endured by life knowing it must die. Even as our personality awakens to the soul's timeless and unchanging realm of joyous blossoming, our soul explores the heights and depths of mortal existence. This conscious interchange of experience is the primary means by which the personality and soul become united in a marriage of Memory and Understanding that outlives the death of the body.

True power is the power to encourage and inspire all that we touch.

By benefiting all that we touch, we benefit the Whole. When we benefit the Whole, we consciously align ourselves with the direction and momentum of *the intention of the Whole*. For the soul, this alignment is as physical a sensation as the body diving into a deep river, swimming underwater, being carried along by the strength and purpose of the current flowing toward its goal.

This stands in stark contrast to the behavior of the personality, which, for most of us, does not trust the flow of the current and so struggles to exert its self-interest by swimming against it. This lack of trust in *the intention of the Whole* accounts for the tragedies in the life of the individual and civilization both: straining against the natural harmony underlying all things, we make a mess of things—placing our own interests ahead of others, we fight the current to the detriment of all.

All that we touch—this points at the edges of our sphere of awareness, how we become more sensitive to the act of communing with other spheres of awareness, and how the edges of our sphere of awareness are constantly growing to touch an ever-widening field of other spheres. Immersing ourselves in the current of *the intention of the Whole*, we come into contact with other spheres of awareness whose Understanding and Memory not only mirror and complement our own but increase and enrich our sensitivity to the nature of the Living Whole. This is called *collaborating with allies at a distance*.

True power, therefore, is also the power to be encouraged and inspired by all that touches us.

For the soul, this *dwelling in the source of encouragement and inspiration* is as physical a sensation as digging a well down to where it taps into the unseen river running under ground. As physical a sensation as the water under ground bubbling up through the well and spilling over its lip to form a stream that nourishes all it touches.

> *I am a well of happiness,*
> *overflowing into the lives of others.*

As the personality becomes more familiar with the deeper feelings that the Third Emanation evokes, it merges with the underlying harmony of the world, like a raindrop falling into a river, and reflects that sense of universal goodwill and well-being in every thought, feeling, and deed.

The practice of *The Five Emanations* is one of self-transformation that is triggered by controlling what we can authentically control—our thoughts. Because our thoughts are rooted in language—we cannot even *think* without putting our thoughts in words—it is essential to pay attention to the way we use language and the way it affects us.

For example, we seldom give a second thought to the sentence, *I am happy*, which is similar to all such statements about emotional states: *I am sad, I am angry, etc.* Here we are using the word "am" to talk about a strictly transitory state—we know that the state we are talking about will change. *I am happy* will not last forever and sooner or later will be replaced by another ephemeral emotion.

What is interesting about this is that other transitory states we experience are described very differently. Take illnesses, for instance, which we know will not last. *I have a cold* or *I have a sprained ankle.* Clearly, we would never think to say, *I am a cold* or *I am a sprained ankle.* How would that make us feel about ourselves? What would I be saying if I caught a cold that I knew would pass and yet identified it as myself, stating, *I am a cold*?

Yet this is exactly what we do with emotions. Instead of correctly identifying transient emotional states by saying *I have happy feelings* or *I have sad feelings* as we would if we were talking about a cold or sprained ankle, we act as if we *are* the emotional state and not simply experiencing a fleeting feeling. The problem, of course, is that in the common usage of the personality I say *I am happy* when things are going my way and *I am sad* when things are going against me.

But how we use language is not as important as how it affects us.

It benefits us greatly to say *I have a cold* because it reminds us that a time is coming when *I no longer have a cold*.

It is to our detriment to say *I am happy* when what we mean is *I am allowing my inner state to be dictated by circumstances that are beyond my control*. Not only am I *happy* because things are going my way but it is often the case that *I am happy* because other people are doing what I want. So *I am sad* or *I am angry* often means *I am allowing my inner state to be dictated by others' actions that are beyond my control*. This is to our detriment because we are pretending we *are* these emotions even though we are fully aware that our inner state will change as soon as outer conditions change.

This is the precise opposite of power.

It is one of the principle ways that the personality disempowers itself.

If the goal is to make our inner state completely vulnerable and at the mercy of the whims of whatever happens to us, then this is certainly the quickest road there.

If, on the other hand, the goal is an inner state that is creative, well-balanced, and capable of exerting a beneficial influence on circumstances and people when the occasion arises, then we need to take the road that empowers the personality.

I am a well of happiness, overflowing into the lives of others.

Each of the five Emanations is a *soul-statement* we use to teach the personality a new way of speaking and, in so doing, a new way of thinking and feeling. Rather than allowing the personality to be trapped in the endless repetition of self-defeating words, we train it to repeat the self-transforming words originating from within the soul's dwelling place. In this way, we shift the personality's perceptions, granting it access to the soul's dwelling place beneath the surface illusion of appearances, just as we can learn to re-focus our gaze to see through the sky's reflection on the pond's surface in order to see the real living universe in the pond's depths.

The soul is itself happiness.

It is not happy one moment, sad the next, angry the next, and so on, depending on whether things are going its way or not.

Its unbounded joy is that of a living being aware of its indestructible *belonging-together* with all other beings making up the indivisible Living Mystery carrying us all from an unimaginable past to an unimaginable future. Aware of the love out of which the universe was—and is—created, the soul has no response but to pour out bliss into the universe surrounding it with love.

In this, the soul is not so different from the personality: both are mysteries to themselves within the greater Mystery. Where they do differ in this regard is in their degree of sensitivity to the communion, to the *belonging-together*, that binds all of Creation together in a single, eternal, act of love.

I am a well of happiness,
overflowing into the lives of others.

Replacing the personality's self-centered way of thinking and feeling with the soul's outpouring of goodwill and well-being, we pass the halfway point in *The Five Emanations* course. Consistently repeating the Third Emanation to ourselves invests us with the inner power to return to the center of the compass points, poised to explore the universe of opportunities before us without losing our bearings within the sacredness of everything.

THE FOURTH EMANATION

LUCK

I am part of a Living Whole
that wants the best for me and all others at the same time.

In a world of uncontrollable events and ever-increasing competition, what is it that brings lasting good fortune?

Being water.

Not being *like* water. *Being* water.

The adult human body is composed of roughly 60% water. An infant's body, a staggering 80%. Our blood is 90% water, while our brain and muscles 75%. Our lungs are about 90% water and even our bones are more than 20%. Our skin, in constant contact with the world around us, is nearly 50% water.

Recognizing the water nature of our physical bodies is a necessary first step, which ought to lead to consciously accepting the degree to which we *are* water. Concentrating on this awareness can likewise move us forward into actually *sensing* the tides and currents of our bodies. Beyond this, then, we can cultivate the sensation of merging with all the other water in the world like a drop of water merging with the ocean of life.

But *being water* cannot be realized from a solely physical perspective. We need to understand the *meaning* of water— we need to penetrate its spirit.

The Grand Cycle of Good Fortune

Our personality needs to merge with the soul of water—

- Every drop of water in the ocean tastes of salt.
- When the ocean's water evaporates to form great rainclouds, each drop must leave behind its salt and become freshwater.
- The wind blows the rain-bearing clouds onto land, where they gather against mountains to loose their cargo of rain that progresses from rivulets to streams to rivers on its way back to the ocean.
- The instant the river empties into the ocean, each drop immediately regains its taste of saltwater.
- When the river empties into the sea, its freshwater carries sediment into the ocean, which adds to its ever-increasing quantity of salt.
- Although all beings living in the ocean live on saltwater, all beings living on land depend utterly on freshwater for life.

Being water depends entirely on seeing water's cycle, point by point, as our soul's mirror—

- While in the Sphere of Universal Communion, we each possess the Understanding and Memory of our true source.

- When we depart for the land of the living, we must each leave behind our conscious Understanding and Memory of our true source.
- When we are born into the land of the living, we join with a body and begin the journey of mortal experience that forms the personality.
- The instant death empties us back into the Sphere of Universal Communion, we each immediately regain our Understanding and Memory of our true source.
- When death empties us back in to the Sphere of Universal Communion, our personalities carry new Memory and Understanding, which adds to the ever-increasing number of its souls.
- Although all beings in the Sphere of Universal Communion depend on Understanding and Memory for their immortality, all beings in the land of the living depend utterly on our personalities for their well-being.

The Three Natural Strategies of Water

Because this final point above identifies the personality as this world's freshwater, it places a great responsibility on us and spurs us to look for a complementary natural law that establishes a solid working model of how our personalities might authentically live —

- In its journey from rivulet to river, water follows the path of least resistance.
- Although water can be terribly destructive in its extremes of drought and flood, its essential nature is to nourish all it touches.
- In its journey from raindrop to sea, water fills up every low place shunned by others as useless and turns it into an oasis of well-being.

As a living mirror of our personalities, then, the nature of water teaches us that—

- We need to make our way through the labyrinth of pathways in this lifetime by consistently choosing the path of nonresistance.
- We need to overcome the terrible destructiveness resulting from the extremes of our apathy and zealotry by consistently keeping in mind and acting on our intrinsic goodwill toward all.
- We need to make our way through the maze of opportunities in this lifetime by looking for opportunities to conscientiously turn situations of *unmet needs* into wellsprings of benefit.

Being water brings lasting good fortune. This is because water *is* good fortune in this world. It is the life-giver and life-sustainer. From sea to clouds to rain and back to sea, it is the grand cycle of *good fortune for all*. Identifying with water—realizing that we *are* water—and acting in accord with its essential nature brings us into harmony with the grand cycle, allowing us to enjoy our allotted portion of good fortune.

I am part of a Living Whole
that wants the best for me and all others at the same time.

Once we have identified with water and have a real sense of our lifetime in the grand cycle, we then concentrate on the three natural strategies that assure lasting good fortune—

- First and foremost, we do not go against the current of the grand cycle of good fortune for all by actively seeking our own success. This kind of self-interest feels like an ulterior motive to the Living Whole and registers as *resistance* to the current of universal good fortune. The practice of *nonresistance* runs deeper, however. It also implies training our personality to allow thoughts, emotions, and memories to simply pass through awareness without any of the friction that causes them to lodge there and become self-defeating habits. The First Emanation, Reflection, is extremely useful in the process of deciding between what has value and what does not.

So, on the external level, it is a question of *righteous intent*. While we go about the performance of our endeavors, we do not concentrate on the results or rewards that might bring. Our intention, rather, is focused exclusively on the benefits it might bring to the whole. Every act, in this sense, is *dedicated* to the well-being of all. Sincerity, which grows with each repetition of the Fourth Emanation, is the hallmark of those having no ulterior motives.

On the internal level, on the other hand, it is a matter of progressively reducing intentions—what has been called *intending not-intending*. The more we cease intending, the less we engage in the internal dialogue. By no longer silently talking to ourselves, we quiet the habit-mind of the personality so that the Understanding of the soul can be heard. This is called *clearing away the weeds so that the flowers might bloom*. This kind of internal non-resistance leads to a profound peace of mind that allows us to sense the direction and momentum of the flow of events without any conscious effort or attempt at reasoning things out.

•   Secondly, we need to recognize the extremes of our self-destructive habits: between a deficit of compassion and an excess of passion, we contribute not only to our own misfortune but set up counter-currents to the good fortune of the whole. By shedding acquired habits that cover over our intrinsic nature, we revert to our original character, which has only goodwill toward all. The middle path here lies in the degree of care, generosity, and loving-kindness appropriate to the situation.

• Lastly, we need to keep in mind that stagnant water breeds an entirely different type of life than does running water. From this, we know that it is better to keep moving, to keep exploring, to ride the living crest of the wave with all the excitement and enthusiasm of the traveler forever setting eyes on the new.

In a world of uncontrollable events and ever-increasing competition, nothing fails like arriving after the wave has already broken. The trick is to arrive at a juncture of positive opportunities before they become apparent to others—to establish your position long before the wave even begins to form. The time-proven method of achieving this is to recognize situations where there are legitimate needs going unmet and to respond to them in an innovative way that ennobles and benefits all concerned. This is a strategy that not only benefits those in need but improves our own opportunities by building a foundation from which to expand into related arenas. This is called *digging a well before the village is even imagined*. It is the way to create good luck, whether the road ahead appears open or closed.

I am part of a Living Whole
that wants the best for me and all others at the same time.

Replacing the personality's intrusive thoughts of self-interest by consciously concentrating on the Fourth Emanation draws us into *accord with the single intent of universal benefit* flowing through the grand cycle of good fortune. We stop placing our own interests ahead of others and begin tying our interests to theirs. We stop concerning ourselves with whether or not we are being taken advantage of and initiate endeavors that work to the advantage of others. We stop distrusting the world and begin experiencing it as a living ocean of loving-kindness and infinite blessings for us all.

Concentrating on the Fourth Emanation opens up our heart-mind to the meanings locked within it. No longer do we count on cleverness or goals to guide our endeavors. As we move ever more in sync with the intent of the Living Whole, our life becomes increasingly improvisational—we find ourselves following the trail of coincidences, accidents, and dreams. This is called *following the prints of a mythical animal back to its secret lair*. But the mythical animal, as it turns out, is real: the creative, fulfilling, and beneficial life, wild and undomesticated as ever, can, nonetheless, be approached and befriended. By treating our life as an unfathomable mystery within a greater mystery, we begin to experience our intuition more as if it were instinct. We move in a heuristic way, finding our way *by feel*, arriving at the right place at the right time, discovering our life-path as if it were inevitable.

We employ a strategy of living without strategies. We empty ourselves of design. We shed the ulterior motives of the personality to make room for the higher aspirations of the soul. This is called *making a nest for the phoenix*. Constantly renewing ourselves by wishing for—and enjoying—the success of others, we abandon self-interest in favor of collective change for the better. In this way, we tie our fortune to the rising tide of good fortune for all. This is called *making a lodging-place for luck*.

Whenever we run into dead ends or frustrations, no matter how great or small, we use the Fourth Emanation to grant us a new vision of the unfolding moment, to set our feet back on the path forward, to uproot us from the dream of confusion and throw us bodily into the reality of bright sunlit mystery. Concentrating on the Fourth Emanation opens our senses to the nature of *belonging together* that lies at the heart of Creation. It wreaks havoc with our illusion of a life separate from other lives and reawakens us to the real world of the *all-at-onceness* of the Living Whole. Why does repeating the Fourth Emanation to ourselves bring lasting good luck? Because in ways untrackable and unfathomable, it echoes the very voice of the Living Whole, calling to It as the conch calls back to the sea. This is called *the chick pecking from within the shell, the hen answering by pecking from without.*

The Living Whole answers those who love it in return.

Placing others ahead of ourselves, promoting their need and advancing their cause, we arrive at the point where we are, truly, *being water.* It is at this turning point that we instinctively and spontaneously embody the single intent of the Living Whole by bringing good luck to all we touch.

This is called *being luck.*

And it is the meaning of the ancient saying, *The rain god does not go begging for a drink of water.*

THE FIFTH EMANATION

CHARISMA

Because everything is sacred,
so am I.

Because *everything* has the same origin, because *everything* is made of the same material, and because *everything* is one single creation, it stands to reason: if *one* thing has a soul, then *every* thing has a soul. This view returns us to the most ancient and universal experience of the world: *matter itself is spirit.* For many millennia, this has been the view shared by indigenous people everywhere. It might be further expressed as, *Because I have an invisible spiritual half, then everything else must likewise possess an invisible spiritual half.*

The validity of this view is found only in experience. If I treat everything as dead spiritless matter, that is how it responds to me. If, on the other hand, I treat everything as living spirit, that is how it responds to me. The fundamental *sameness* of all creation results in a fundamental equality that demands of us that we treat everything with equal respect and dignity. And it demands that we train ourselves to become ever more sensitive to the nobility of the soul within all.

This perspective endures to the present day. There still exist peoples who know that if one thing in the world is considered to be a *person*, then every thing must be considered to be a *person*. Human beings, of course, are persons. But so are animal-persons. And river-persons. And mountain-persons. And plant-persons. Addressing each thing in creation as a *person* helps train us to become ever more sensitive to the immortal soul within all.

And this fundamental *sameness* of all creation means, of course, that I need to train myself to become ever more sensitive to the nobility of the immortal soul within me.

There are two kinds of charisma—visible and invisible.

Visible charisma emanates from the personality and attracts other people to our alliance. It is based on the sense of sacredness we come to embody: once we feel our own person to be as sacred as all the rest of creation, we hold ourselves differently and speak differently and react to life differently. That difference is the inner dignity and nobility we experience as the center from which all our thoughts and words and actions flow.

Invisible charisma emanates from the soul and attracts other souls to our alliance. It is based on our sensitivity to the sacredness of all creation: once we feel our surroundings to be filled with other spheres of aware light, we consciously lean into the coming moment in the most ennobling manner possible. With such sensitivity, the coming moment ceases to loom with potential difficulties and comes to mark the immovable site of the dignity and nobility of all souls.

We attract other people when we accept our own nobility, in other words, and we attract other souls when we consciously ennoble everything that touches us. *Accepting our own nobility* means that we ennoble our every thought, word and action. *Ennobling everything that touches us* means that we do not hold ourselves apart from the divinity pouring out of every aspect of creation.

Charisma is called *visible* when it pertains to the visible world of the body, whereas it is called *invisible* when it pertains to the invisible world of the soul.

Visible charisma blossoms when we look into our light-half instead of our shadow-half. Why do we find it easier to look into our shadow-half than into the bright and pure nature of our light-half? Because our shadow gives us a comfortable excuse for falling short of fulfilling our potential. Gazing into our radiant half and recognizing its innate nobility as our own, after all, extinguishes all our self-defeating habits of thought as instantaneously as flipping a switch replaces the dark of a room with light. Our pure and radiant nature? Yes: that with which we are born and to which we must return.

We embody visible charisma when we stop doubting our own sacredness.

Invisible charisma blossoms when we treat other souls as immortal, wise, and loving entities possessing profound Understanding and Memory to share. This way of being-with other souls needs to be thought of as *soul-to-soul* interaction and not something we can imitate with our personalities. It comes from our soul and addresses all the other souls who touch us.

In this light, we have to keep in mind that not all souls are associated with human beings—they likewise imbue every form of matter, whether animal, plant, or mineral, with its invisible spiritual half. Beyond that, however, it is also necessary to keep in mind that that not all souls are immediately associated with any particular form of matter— they exist in the timeless and dimensionless *Sphere of Universal Communion* to which your own soul has constant access. So it is not just a matter of listening to the teachings of the soul within all of nature. It is also a matter of sensing the presence of those disembodied souls who care enough about the living to share the teachings of their Understanding and Memory with us.

We embody invisible charisma when we stop doubting the sacredness of all that is beyond our senses.

When we speak of an alliance, we are speaking about relationships of lasting mutual benefit.

It may be friendship, love, family, a business enterprise, a creative endeavor, or even a large-scale cause with social, political, or spiritual goals. But what authentic alliances all have in common is that all members are treated as the sacred being of unknown potential they in reality are.

Real charisma *creates* mutual benefit—not by force of personality but by transparency of personality. It allows the invisible half to shine through the visible half. It allows the immortal to shine through the mortal. It allows the innate nobility of the soul to shine through the social conditioning of the personality. It calls forth from others their very best.

Real charisma spreads throughout the alliance, calling forth and enhancing the natural charisma of every member.

The *purpose* of charisma is to draw others, both visible and invisible, to help with our lifework. The *function* of charisma is to answer the call of others, both visible and invisible, for help with their lifework.

To be charismatic is not simply to be blessed, after all.

To be charismatic is also to bless.

The Charisma of Sincerity

No one can "act" charismatic. It is not something that can be feigned or imitated.

Real charisma flows spontaneously and un-self-consciously from the soul's shining act of self-remembering. Understanding the way in which the personality is formed by childhood experiences and then cultivated during adulthood, the soul takes up the work of clarifying the purpose of this lifetime by giving the personality a vision of its highest potential. Because the personality is not a fixed and concrete entity but, rather, a set of habits that are easier to disrupt than is generally imagined, the soul makes use of this openness to transform the personality by revealing its transparency to it. This is called *two bright mirrors facing one another*.

Simply by interrupting the flow of the personality's habit-thoughts with its own self-remembering, the soul triggers the personality's metamorphosis into a reflection of instant communion. When the personality comes to reflect the sacredness of everything, it affects others by its very being— they immediately recognize their own essence in its presence and open themselves to a relationship of lasting mutual benefit. This is called *emerging from the cocoon in a field of butterflies*.

When personality and soul are united, the person's sincere dedication to the sacredness of everything draws people into an alliance that enriches and ennobles the lifetime of each. We cannot strive for real charisma, we cannot pretend we sense the sacredness uniting us with the Living Whole. Real charisma is simply the natural side effect of personally experiencing the union of the soul and personality in this lifetime. This is called *having a mind within the mind, having a body outside the body*.

The Charisma of Absurdity

The only problem with Truth is that it is completely indistinguishable from its opposite.

Charisma does not necessarily express itself as serious and meaningful. It also demonstrates a streak of playfulness that aims to open up thought to new possibilities, seeking to spark the imagination and provoke appreciation of the incongruities of life. It looks at our patterns of thought and reactions and finds the humor in the borderland between expectations and the unexpected.

Nasruddin, the holy fool, entered a bar and asked the bartender, "Have you ever seen me before?" The bartender looked at him closely before replying, "No, never." Nasruddin raised an eyebrow. "Then how do you know it's me?" he demanded suspiciously.

Enlightenment is the last refuge of the unenlightened.

Those who integrate their light half do not automatically fall into the stereotype of saintly behavior. In fact, many integrate it in equal measure with their shadow half, producing a world view full of paradox and self-contradiction. Real charisma does not take on the stereotypical trappings of holiness. Real enlightenment does not fall into the trap of enlightenment. Such a distorted preconception explains why so many people hesitate to step onto the path of self-transformation: they fear they will not be able to live up to their own expectations of saintly behavior.

Nasruddin went on a pilgrimage and, in the course of the long journey, lost his favorite copy of the Koran. It was the only thing to mar the memory of the pilgrimage and, as the years went by, he often regretted misplacing it along the way.

One day while he was standing by his garden gate, a goat approached, carrying a book in his mouth. Nasruddin took the book from the goat and gasped in astonishment as he realized it was his long-lost Koran. "It's a miracle, for my favorite has returned to me!" he cried. "Not really," explained the goat, "your address is written on the inside."

Absurdity is the highest form of metaphysics.

Charisma mirrors the profoundly mysterious nature of this sacred creation and finds the laughter in the unpredictable twists and turns of our way of looking at things. Every drop in the river may obey the over-arching law of falling along the line of gravity toward the sea, but the behavior of none can be predicted with absolute accuracy at any given moment. They swirl, leap, reverse course in countercurrents, pause in stagnant pools, rush through rapids, all in the chance-driven randomness of moment-to-moment exceptions to the rule. Just like human beings. We are all passing from birth to death but our individual stories intertwine in a living tapestry of infinite jest and eternal surprise.

One day Nasruddin and his friend went fishing. They rented a boat and started out before dawn. Getting disoriented in the dark, they stumbled upon a new location where the fish nearly jumped into their boat. They fished all day, laughing and congratulating themselves for the best catch of their lives. Reluctantly, they raised anchor and turned toward home as the sun threatened to set. No sooner did the harbor come into view, however, than Nasruddin slapped his forehead and exclaimed, "Oh, we should have marked that spot! How will we ever find it again?" His friend waved him off reassuringly. "Not to worry," he said, "I carved a mark here on the rail of the boat where it was so we could find our way back." Nasruddin stared at his friend incredulously. "You fool!" he cried. "What if they rent us a different boat?"

The trickster, the jester, the comic, the holy fool. This form of charisma does not need the sacred to always make sense, for it revels in the unexpected that comes disguised as nonsense.

This is called *seeing like an eagle in the day and like a jaguar in the night.*

The Charisma of Magic

There is a kind of charisma that is unfathomable even to the soul who possesses it.

This results in a kind of knowing without knowing how one knows.

And a kind of acting without anticipating the results of one's actions.

In practice, this feels as though we act without any cause — and without any preconception of what effects might result from our actions. We seem to be following the scent of an elusive prey that others have forgotten even exists. This is called *engaging with the heart of a child, disengaging with the wisdom of an elder.*

We shouldn't mistake such idiosyncratic behavior for addled-mindedness: the non-rational behavior of such a person is of the highest order. Nearly anyone can learn to behave in a rational and socially coherent manner, after all. The charisma of magic does not extinguish our ability to act responsibly, of course — rather, it raises it to a higher order of reason, a transcendent reason that acts on the *causes underlying everything at the same time* and produces *effects that appear in other times and places.* It expresses our responsibility to the Living Whole. But because we cannot envision or comprehend the entirety of the Whole, our responsibility as one of its parts is likewise beyond our ken. The Living Whole expresses itself *through us* when we accept our own mysterious and unknowable nature—when we accept our own sacred mystery as part of the sacred mystery of everything. This is called *attuning your voice to the celestial choir.*

At this point, the personality has essentially replaced its old habits of thought with the soul's. Sacredness itself becomes a habit, slips beneath the threshold of conscious knowledge, and merges with the subliminal unanimous act of creation. The soul's Understanding shines through—not the bright sunlight of noonday but the soft moonlight of midnight—in an unconditional acceptance of its *belonging* to the present moment. This is why the ancients say, *All the differences stand out in the light, all the differences become one in the dark.*

To such a person, the whole world is magic.

Just as there is only one Formless, there is only one Form.

It is as if the Living Whole divided into two halves, the Formless and the Form, who in turn created spirit and matter. From this perspective, each thing in creation is a microcosm of the Living Whole, each with its own sacred duality of soul and body. Out of this mix of the Formless and the Form, however, something else emerged: Humanity, which stands perpetually between spirit and matter, straddling them, part of both and yet never one or the other. Each personality is, in this sense, a microcosm of the whole of Humanity, since the personality is the lower soul born from the union of the higher soul and the body. The macrocosmic Great Work of aligning Humanity with the Living Whole, then, may only be accomplished on the microcosmic level when enough individuals recognize the origin of their personality and align it with their soul. Such an alignment may only be accomplished by real persons, who perceive the sacredness of all matter and every soul, stumbling thereby upon the first-hand realization of their own sacredness.

It is as if such real persons materially further the macrocosmic Great Work of triggering the limitless potential of Humanity by unconditionally accepting the unknowable nature of their own sacred mystery.

Just as there is only one Spirit, there is only one Body.

And only one Humanity.

Such real persons stand beside the Gate of Mystery, watching the comings and goings of the formless and form, adapting their lifework to the changing circumstances of the Age. Watching the comings of *the formless taking form* and the goings of *form returning to the formless*, such real persons align themselves with the Unknowable and act without conscious purpose. A well-ordered life, in other words, is attained by achieving a high degree of purposelessness that is based on aligning oneself with the Unknowable standing forever on the other side of the Gate of Mystery.

For such real persons, the whole world is a vessel of charisma.

There is nothing that is not wondrous or awe-inspiring. Nothing that does not draw us into the Great Work. It carries us along with its purpose, so it can only be adapted to and not controlled. It permeates my cells and atoms, so there cannot be even the slightest gap between me and the world. Such a world produces a mind devoid of opposites.

Everything is a circle whose center is everywhere.

Where else could the moment-to-moment mind reside?

One day, Nasruddin, the holy fool, rode his donkey through the marketplace, whipping it into a frenzy, racing it among the booths, overturning goods, knocking patrons into one another, and demanding angrily of everyone he passed, "Who stole my donkey? Who stole my donkey?"

People look everywhere for the One, blaming external circumstances of one kind or the other for their not finding it. Yet it is that which carries them through Life, whether they are aware of it or not. Real persons are those who are aware of it and harmonize with it every moment.

Because everything is sacred, so am I.

AFTERWORD

THE ART OF SELF-AWAKENING

I do not rely on the implications of physics or philosophy or psychology to explain how the Five Emanations change life for the better. Instead, I rely solely on my first-hand experience, both among the living and the dead. In this, I follow in the footsteps of great-souled beings, who long ago recognized that the personality does not exist until the body is born with a soul attached. This spiritual vivification was seen for what it was: the birth of a new soul.

That it was an embryonic *lower soul* dependent on the older *higher soul* for Understanding and Wisdom was to the ancients self-evident. It was for this reason that they designed protocols by which the lower soul could be cultivated in a single lifetime and return with the higher soul to the Sphere of Universal Communion immediately upon the body's death rather than wandering lost and confused in the realm of illusory memory.

The protocols for aligning the lower and higher souls have not changed in essence over the millennia but they have changed dramatically in form so as to accord with the historical epoch in which they appear. All this I have learned through communion with great-souled beings both here among the living and there among the dead.

The Five Emanations is, in this sense, the newest incarnation of those ancient protocols that my teachers feel belong to this historical epoch.

It is a course of self-transformation in the tradition of sudden enlightenment practitioners. It follows in the footsteps of those who empty out their self-defeating patterns of thought, emotion, and memory in order to make a lodging-place for the original uncreated awareness. It points to the shortcut method by which the modern mind of one's contemporaries is permanently aligned with the ancient soul ever-awakening within every form.

In all this, it adheres to the ancient teaching of self-liberation, which transcends the separation of spirit and matter by uniting That Which Is Above with That Which Is Below in this very body and in this very lifetime.

Blessing

You are the Understanding and Memory
That You Emanate

RECAPITULATION

THE FIRST EMANATION: REFLECTION

*As an immortal spirit, are these the thoughts, feelings
and memories I choose for eternity?*

THE SECOND EMANATION: FREEDOM

*What is most important is not how others are treating me —
What is most important is how I am treating others.*

THE THIRD EMANATION: POWER

*I am a well of happiness,
overflowing into the lives of others.*

THE FOURTH EMANATION: LUCK

*I am part of a Living Whole
that wants the best for me and all others at the same time.*

THE FIFTH EMANATION: CHARISMA

*Because everything is sacred,
so am I.*

ABOUT THE AUTHOR

William Douglas Horden

Has researched spiritual traditions of East and West, North and South, for
the past 40 years. He has traveled extensively and lived in various
shamanic communities, steeping himself in the timeless world view of the
ancient cultures. He was initially trained in the I Ching by Master Khigh
Alx Dhiegh and has since developed a new approach to the ancient art.
He currently lives in Southern Oregon.

Other Books by William Douglas Horden

The Toltec I Ching
(with Martha Ramirez-Oropeza)

The Spiritual Basis of Good Fortune
The Intentional Body
Sun Pearl Ceremonial

Made in the USA
Charleston, SC
04 October 2011